If He Doesn't Deliver
Domestic Violence in the Religious Home

MARILYN JOYCE

Copyright © 2016 Marilyn Joyce

All rights reserved.

ISBN: 978-0-9634823-5-8

MJ Media Grp
4115 Columbia Rd, Ste 5359
Martinez, GA 30907 US
www.AuthorMarilynJoyce.com

All rights reserved under International Copyright Law.

Contents and/or cover may not be reproduced in whole or in part in any form without the express written consent of the Publisher: MJMG, 4115 Columbia Rd, Ste 5359, Martinez, Georgia 30907

Unless otherwise indicated, all scripture quotations are taken from the HOLY BIBLE, NEW INTERNATIONAL VERSION. Copyright (c) 1973, 1978 by International Bible Society.

Some scripture quotations are taken from the King James Version of the Bible.

Some scripture taken from THE AMPLIFIED BIBLE. Old Testament copyright (c) 1965, 1987 by The Zondervan Corporation. The Amplified New Testament (c) 1958, 1987 by the Lochman Foundation. Used by permission.

DEDICATION

This book is dedicated to those who have wrestled with the hurt, confusion, pain, and betrayal of abuse.

CONTENTS

Acknowledgements	i
INTRODUCTION	1
Are You Aware?	5
Early Commitment	8
Hearts Divided	12
Hope Deferred	21
You Must Forgive	32
Pray, Pray, Pray	38
Strange Attractions	41
Spirit-filled Counsel	45
Persecuted For His Name Saked	51
INTRODUCTION – SECTION TWO	55
Someone to Confide In	56
A Spirit of Rejection	61
Unwise Counsel	67
Constant Hope	71
Expression of Love?	75
Examine Yourself	77
The Value of a Good Pastor	82
Guard Your Heart	88
Learn To…	92
In Conclusion	95
About the Author	99

ACKNOWLEDGEMENTS

I will always be grateful for my prayer partner, Ezella Karnes Osborn. Those heartbreaking and frank conversations during our evening jogs inspired me to stop procrastinating about writing this book.

While visiting his family in Hawaii, Daniel Hilliard helped me with the grueling typing and proofreading tasks of the first edition of this book. Thank you, Daniel for the selfless investment of your time and talent.

Thank you, Tricia Ready for your inspiration. Your words: 'Be change ready' caught my spirit off guard, but has been the defining word of grace for this new season.

My special thanks to domestic violence shelters, church counseling departments, prison therapists, and small business owners who have used this book over the years to help the communities you serve.

I will always be grateful for Dean Nazaru McCray. You have helped me deal with incredible challenges with supportive attentiveness, encouragement, and tenderness – never allowing me to forget the grace and power of God. Thank you for encouraging me to dream big. Mere words cannot express how much I admire, respect, and appreciate you.

INTRODUCTION

The last time I was slammed against the wall, I realized I was going to lose the baby. As I slid to the floor, I watched him look down at me with what seemed to be contempt. I told him that I needed to get to a hospital, and that I was losing the baby. He simply ran out the door, jumped into the car, and drove away.

I crawled through the den and down the long hall to the bedroom. The children were screaming and crying, but I didn't have the strength to even pick myself up. My head was swimming. I knew I losing consciousness. I didn't want the children to see this.

No, I didn't want an ambulance or any outsiders in my home. What would I say? How could I tell anyone, least of all total strangers, that my husband and pastor had left me to bleed to death in front of our children? There would be lights and police in front of the church parsonage - and this was such a gossiping little town. They would never let the children and I have any peace. There would be questions and whispers and probing for explanations. How do you explain a violent, cruel, and abusive pastor, husband, and father?

As I lost consciousness across my bed, through my mind ran the hardest question of all: where was God?

> **The National Domestic Violence Hotline**
> **1-800-799-7233 OR 1-800-787-3224 (TTY)**

When Christians take vows of matrimony, they enter a divine union. The marriage covenant creates a powerful bond. When someone who really loves God takes those vows, they've made a life long commitment to work as hard as necessary to make that relationship successful, knowing that with Christ as the head, all things are possible.

Imagine what it must feel like to begin to experience problems in that marriage, knowing that your only hope is in God, and yet things are not getting better. Or, worse yet, perhaps your marriage has ended.

You have faith. You have prayed. You have fasted. You have taken authority over the devil. Yet, you find yourself left to somehow try to live through the pain of abuse, rejection, and maybe even death or divorce. This book is written for those hurting sisters and brothers in the body of Christ who have experienced the pain of abuse and/or divorce AS A CHRISTIAN.

My heart's desire for you is that you come to know that the rest of your life does not have to fall apart because the situation may not have turned out the way you prayed it would.

This book is also written for those of you who may know someone who has had this experience and you desire to know what to do about your hurting, disillusioned, (and quite possibly) backslidden sister or brother. Perhaps it is difficult for you to understand why they may still be struggling in their walk with the Lord. Perhaps it is even more difficult for you to understand how pain and confusion can linger so long within them.

In a recent sermon, my pastor said, "One day God is going to ask you, what did you do about your hurting brother and sister? If they're not being helped in the church, they will go out into other places." This is so true.

I meet people all the time, usually women, (but also men), who have given up on themselves and their relationship with God because they've had a painful experience they could not understand. For one reason or another they were not able to find the answers they needed; nor could they find relief and release from the pain.

There are answers to the questions in your heart. You <u>can</u> go on with your life in Christ. God has not abandoned you, and He has not failed you; even though that may very well be what you are feeling. In fact, someone may have told you that you didn't have enough faith, or any of a number of things that may only have caused you to be afraid to even try trusting the Lord with your life again.

<u>God is for you</u>. He really is. And I invite you back into a relationship with Him; a meaningful, workable, day-by-day relationship that will lead you out of the place of wandering and wondering. But, you will have to be willing to allow the Spirit of God to bring you to a place of healing in a very deep and personal way. And, you will also have to be willing to fight for your own restoration.

You may say that you've prayed every prayer, stood in faith, and confessed every promise in the Word of God that is available to you; and still things didn't turn out the way you knew they could have. Don't give up on God or yourself.

Read on!!!

CHAPTER ONE
ARE YOU AWARE?

The statistics on the number of reported battered and abused women in this country are staggering. The National Center for Prevention of Sexual and Domestic Violence (www.ncdsv.org) reports that every 9 seconds a woman is affected by a violent incident. Of all the causes of injury, domestic violence is ranked number one among women. Every six hours, one woman dies as a result of a violent incident.

In light of these statistics, it is almost impossible *not* to know someone who is, or has been, a victim of some form of abuse. With this in mind, it is imperative for the Christian who desires to be an instrument of God's healing touch in the world around them, to come to understand the needs of fellow Christians dealing with this issue.

It took me 10 years to be able to openly share about how God brought me out of the nightmare of a violent and abusive marriage. Almost every time I've shared my testimony, I've been approached later by people who seem to be surprised to find out that there are Christians who are experiencing abuse. Yet, after several minutes of conversation, they usually end up sharing their personal knowledge of someone who is living with some form of abuse.

Likewise, when I'm ministering, it surprises me how many women and men talk with me after the service to share and pray about their own abusive experiences. There are so many hurting people in our midst!! Many ask me, "How can this happen in a Christian family?" The problem of abuse affects people from all walks of life, both in and out of the pews. Keep in mind the fact that in many aspects the church is like any organization that consists of people from all walks of life. Like I always say, *where ever there are people, there are people problems.*

This is not the time for us to be shocked. Too many of us know that abuse is already a problem. Instead, this is the time for us, the church, to began to rise up and take responsibility for cleaning ourselves up. We need to look within, as well as around ourselves, and make a decisive commitment to an attitude that ministers healing.

Pretending the problem doesn't exist isn't going to make it go away. Whether we are willing to admit it or not, battery does go on in Christian homes. God does not want us to learn to live with it. He wants us to live free from it - both the abused and the abuser.

I've met so many women who have left the church because of the devastation of experiencing abuse at the hands of a husband who was supposed to be a Christian. The rejection and mistreatment they experienced became a catalyst in a process, designed by the enemy, to push them away from their very relationship with the Lord.

Because of abuse, I felt that the bed-chambers of my own relationship with the Lord had been invaded and ripped apart, and that I would never again be able to enter into that place of protection and safety I had always known.

Since that time, I have come to realize that I am God's masterpiece. The incredible scars of that experience required that He do His best work of molding and reshaping my life. After an injurious interruption and infringement by the enemy on the masterpiece that God was creating, which was my life, God began to rebuild the walls of my character and personality.

My husband was not only my mate, friend, and companion; he was also my pastor. We stood together in ministry leadership. Because of that fact, I had the experience of meeting many women, from every walk of life, who were also experiencing abuse. It would be impossible to address every woman's experience. I can only share the experiences of women I've known, counseled, and prayed with, as well as my own.

CHAPTER TWO
EARLY COMMITMENT

My initial experience with Christ is perhaps, not much different from many others. I accepted Christ as my personal Savior when I was nine years old. Several months later, while standing on the sidewalk watching as my father (who was in the military) depart for Panama. I was overwhelmed with a new awareness of how much of a difference Christ had already made in my life. I realized that my feelings toward my family were different. Different and deeper.

I began to realize that I loved them. I mean I *really* loved them in a way I knew I was not capable of on my own. For the first time I was becoming aware of God's love being poured out to others through me. There was an obvious difference between the love that I had previously and the love of God which was now at work in me.

It was such a tremendous difference until, even though I was only nine, I realized, in the light of God's love, that I never really loved my family. This love, the love that God gave was so real, so powerful, and so far above anything I could ever describe.

During the years that followed, I learned that God's love is the birthmark of the believer. Jesus said: *"By this all men will know that you are my disciples, if you love one another" (John 13:35 NIV).*

The word for "love" in this scripture, "*agape*" is the same word used in 1 John 4:8, which says, **"...God is love."** Agape. The love that is God.

1 Corinthians 13, says that I can have mountain-moving faith, have all knowledge, speak in tongues, or can even give myself as a human sacrifice; but, if I don't have love, all of that means nothing, and I am nothing. The love of God is the most essential element of the Christian life.

At the age of nine, I didn't understand all of that. I could not even imagine how these truths would impact my life. I only knew that Jesus was my Friend and Savior. I had the love of God in my heart, and I could tell Him anything. I simply decided that I would be honest with the Lord about what I thought and felt - even if it wasn't very nice.

When I was happy, sad, lonely, joyful, depressed, anxious, confident, fearful, etc., I told Him all about it. Even though I began to hear people say not to "confess" negative feelings; my attitude was: God is our Father and we ought to be able to talk to Him as the Father that He is. We can't deceive Him, lying to Him serves no purpose, so why can't we simply tell Him everything? A psychiatrist once told me that they are paid thousands of dollars a year by people who, many times, simply need to talk to someone who will listen. We need to learn that we can tell God whatever we have on our hearts.

He is interested. He will not only listen, but He will also act on our behalf. Being honest before God about what I was thinking, feeling, and experiencing brought me through the ordeal of an abusive marriage. It was a particularly hard chapter of my life because the situation made me feel that I had been abandoned by God. Those feelings of abandonment shook my relationship with the Lord for several years. It took some time for me to realize that God had never left me, nor has He left you.

I know that many who have experienced the pain and tragedy of abuse will read the following pages and identify with the experience. I say to you, be honest before God and allow Him to do a complete healing work in your life. Being honest before Him is what brought healing in me. A healing work that goes on for me, even today.

Before I can share my experience, I must start at the beginning. Sixth grade is where everything concerning my walk with the Lord really began for me. I grew up in a military family and we were stationed at Fort Benning, Georgia at the time.

There was an excellent director of our Sunday school who had a great impact on my life. Each Sunday morning, the sixth graders gathered for a general assembly that took place before and after the Sunday school classes. Many times that general assembly was the most fascinating place I'd been all week.

My heart raced as this talented woman opened the Bible up to us through visual aids and felt boards. You could have heard a pin drop as she shared the Bible events: the life of Moses, Jesus and His disciples, Naaman, etc., as well as the lives of various missionaries. Her presentations were very interesting and organized as she placed each figure on the felt board. She never failed to make each event personal and challenging.

As she shared about how missionary families served Jesus against all odds, even with the threat of death, it was settled in my heart that I would one day be a missionary. Not just any missionary, but a missionary nurse that one day would face enemy soldiers, communists, or some unknown enemy, who would look me in the eye and demand that I denounce Christ or lose all. And, of course, I would never denounce Him. I would be miraculously delivered by God's unseen hand, time and time again. However, I would always be prepared to give up everything for the cause of Christ.

Well, I grew older, and although I was a part of youth missionary groups, and even had the chance to meet real missionaries, the opportunity for me to become a foreign missionary never presented itself. The Lord called me to be a Bible teacher, and a nurse, both of which I pursued.

I was taught well. I was taught that being a Christian meant to be a witness, and being a witness also meant to be willing to lay down your life. In other words, I was fully persuaded that my commitment to Christ meant everything. I was fully prepared to one day be given the choice to choose Christ or lose all on foreign soil. I never expected to have to make that choice in my own home.

CHAPTER THREE
HEARTS DIVIDED

I wanted a deeper walk with the Lord. I wanted the opportunity to serve Him full-time and to share my faith without restraint. I wanted my children raised in a power-packed, Holy Spirit filled environment, and after several years of prayer, God granted that desire.

Soon after our marriage, my husband began to pastor. No longer did I have to hear a supervisor say it was against the rules "to discuss politics or religion on the job". Talking about Jesus was our job. It was wonderful!

I never wearied of reading and studying the Word and ministering to others. The Lord always had us off on one adventure or another. It was exciting to see the enemy defeated by our powerful and awesome God!

I began to lie on the floor on my face before God when I woke each morning. There I would pray and then read the Word for an hour or more. The Holy Spirit would deal with me heavily during the night as well, and I would go across the parking lot to the church and spend hours in prayer and communion with my sweet Savior. Many times my husband would join me. Those were the most refreshing and exciting times for me.

I couldn't imagine trying to live life without this intimate fellowship with the Lord. A real relationship with the Lord is an intimate one. Acts 17:28 says: ***"For in Him*** (the Lord) *we live and move and have our being."*

Before we were married, I told my husband that Christ was my life and if we could not share my Life, then we could have no life together. It was a blessing to have a husband who understood and shared that intimacy.

> *Do two walk together unless they have agreed to do so? Amos 3:3 (NIV)*

The church was growing and, at the same time, we began to discover that some of our congregation had grown up in and still practiced witchcraft or some form of satanism. We quickly learned that it was a common practice for these people to be assigned to churches in order to hinder the move of God and to stir up trouble - and stir up trouble they did!

In addition, we discovered that many (teenagers and adults alike) had problems with both illegal and prescription drugs. Therefore, my husband began to preach a great deal about the power of the Holy Spirit.

We came under vicious attack very soon after that. I was frequently telephoned by certain members of the congregation who would use the foulest profanities in telling me how they didn't appreciate what he was preaching.

The more my husband ministered in these areas, especially when he ministered about the power of the Holy Spirit, the more problems key people involved in these activities would try to create for us.

There were attempts to poison us, death threats, and of course, the old favorite game of the enemy, which is to spread lies, accusations, and gossip about the pastor and his family in an attempt to discredit the ministry.

Among other things, I was accused of being a lesbian and my husband a homosexual. There were also allegations rumored that we seduced the young people during the youth Bible studies (ages 13-25) we held in our home each week. The mother that started the rumor later admitted that she had done so because she had much rather have her daughter be thought of as a lesbian than the "religious fanatic" she felt her daughter had become.

While attending our church, her daughter had graduated high school and was attending college. She was active in the choir, attended the weekly youth Bible studies at the church, was an honor student, had a part-time job, spent hours a day in prayer, shared Jesus with her friends and family, and was engaged to a minister. Countless young people came to the Lord and came off drugs through her bold witness.

Needless to say, there were parents that believed the rumors anyway and forbade their children to associate with us, or to attend the youth Bible studies. Teenagers would literally sneak to our home and meet us after church for prayer to receive the Lord, or the baptism of the Holy Spirit. (For those of you who didn't know it, persecutions of this type are common place in the lives of pastors and their families.)

Since we were under constant attack and pressure, there were times we were not sure just how to respond to the things which were happening to us. We didn't want to operate in the flesh. Instead, we wanted God's wisdom and

His perfect will for everything we did and said.

The easiest response would have been to retaliate in anger under the circumstances. But we wanted to see people saved and set free, no matter how much the enemy tried to hinder us.

For those reasons, we chose to rely totally upon the Holy Spirit for direction, and constantly stayed before the Lord so that we could walk in love, and in the right attitude.

This caused us to develop a tremendous prayer life.

> **Therefore confess your sins to each other and pray for each so that you may be healed. The prayer of a righteous person is powerful and effective.**
> **James 5:16 (NIV)**

We began to see awesome miracles take place. One thing we knew for sure: God had called us to this work, and He was more powerful than any force of the enemy. He had to be in control. We saw victory after victory as people began to give their hearts to the Lord and denounce witchcraft. We also began to see victories over drug addiction. People were being set free and their lives were being turned around.

Yet, even as we witnessed awesome miracles and victories in the lives of those we were ministering to, after a time, it seemed as though my very enthusiasm about what God was doing in our ministry became a source of conflict in our marriage. At first, it was easy to denounce this as a lie from the enemy. But, as time passed, there was no denying the sense of "spiritual competition" where there had once been mutual rejoicing over what God was doing in our lives.

At the dinner table, we usually shared something from the Bible such as a scripture, or a thought from our personal Bible study time that had really blessed us that day, or a testimony. But, instead of the excitement I was accustomed to, there was now anger and outrage.

After Bible study sessions with the ministers' wives or the youth group, if there were reports of demonstrations of the Spirit, if a word of knowledge was confirmed, if someone received the baptism of the Holy Spirit, or if a healing had taken place; my husband would accuse me of attempting to make him look bad as a minister.

Other crazy accusations were: "You think you're God." Or "You think you can tell God what to do," or similar nonsense, and then he would become violent.

There had been a few violent episodes in the past, but now those episodes had re-surfaced with a devastating, injurious force, and an alarming frequency. I retaliated by spending hours a day in prayer. Even with two small children, the Lord provided plenty of time alone with Him.

In addition to my early morning and late night prayer vigil, I began spending several more hours a day in prayer after my housework was done and my children were napping. I was becoming increasingly more confused about why this was continuing to happen in what was supposed to be a Christian home.

We knew the Bible. We knew the Word said the thief (satan) comes only to steal, kill, and to destroy (John 10:10). We both knew the Word also says to resist the devil and he will flee (James 4:7). Therefore, I began to pray the Word of God over our situation. I had to do it alone because my husband no longer prayed or read the Word with me. He even began to find other things to do during the time that he normally set aside for his private devotions. I began to wonder if he was reading the Word or praying at all anymore.

As I thought about all the things we had been through and were still experiencing, it occurred to me that perhaps he had gotten discouraged. Being the pastor of such a large church under the stress of the lies, rumors, and accusations was not an easy task. But the violence that he was inflicting upon me was creating quite another problem for us.

It wasn't easy to get him to talk about our problems. We could talk about other things easy enough, but whenever it was a personal matter we had to discuss, he would literally sit there in silence. I remember sitting up with him all night, hoping and praying that he would say something - anything - to give me some insight into what he was really feeling. When he would talk, all he would say was: "Why should we talk? All you're going to do is say: it's all my fault. You want to blame me for everything."

It was like talking to a small child. He was so concerned about who was going to get the blame that he could not admit that he had hurt me or the children. He was not even willing to pray with me about stopping the violence and improving our relationship.

Abusers are usually emotionally immature. They will remain that way as long as they have someone willing to take the blame for their actions. It is much easier for them not to take responsibility for their actions and to carry on with things as if nothing ever happened.

For example, in my case, after every incident, my husband would take me to the mall several days later. Suddenly, he was so sweet. I could have anything I wanted - nothing cost too much. If I refused to go with him he would go shopping alone and bring back a nice ensemble for me to wear to church. Then, he would hug me and say, "I'm sorry" and that was supposed to be the end of it. He was all smiles again. Then he would "carry on" as if nothing had ever happened. If I brought up the subject of the abuse again, he would accuse me of not being satisfied unless I could "keep trouble going."

Abusers usually need someone or something to blame for their actions - again, to avoid taking responsibility. There were times I actually felt that my husband was trying to get me to take responsibility for his abusive behavior by avoiding discussion and focusing the conversation on the phrase "you want to say all of our problems are my fault".

Quite naturally, any marriage partner would automatically respond to a statement like that with an acknowledgment of shared responsibility or "blame" for any problems in the relationship. However, abusers can take advantage of the willingness of the spouse who wants to work on the problem by manipulating them into the position of "taking the blame".

Unfortunately, many women eventually allow themselves to be convinced that they *are* the cause for the abuse. I've actually heard women say that they "deserved" to be battered; that they "somehow brought it on themselves". A neighbor once told me, "If a man doesn't hit you sometimes, he doesn't love you". She was confused.

The Bible says if you don't **spank your children** (as a means of discipline), you don't love them (Proverbs 13:24). There is a definite and distinct difference between a ***child*** and a ***wife***.

The Bible also has some very specific things to say about how a husband should treat his wife:

> *Husbands, love your wives, just as Christ loved the church, and gave Himself for her.*
>
> *In this same way, husbands ought to love their wives as their own bodies. He who loves his wife loves himself.*
>
> *After all, no one ever hated their own body, but they feed and care for their body, just as Christ does the church.*
> *Ephesians 5:25, 28-29 (NIV)*

I tried to avoid taking the blame for my husband's abusive behavior by acknowledging the fact that the abuse was not simply a matter of blame, but it was a problem that was destroying our family. I'd say things like: "we" had a problem; and that "we" needed to get help.

I did not provoke him. I was not the type of person who deliberately did things that I knew would make my husband become violent. In addition, I never felt that I "deserved" to be mistreated.

I didn't understand why the violence was occurring, or exactly what it would take to make it end. But, of this one thing I was very sure: the Bible says, *"If we confess our sins, He is faithful and just and will forgive us our sins and purify us from all unrighteousness" (1 John 1:9 NIV)*.

I was praying for the day when my husband would face his problem honestly and openly before God. That was something he had to do himself. I could not do it for him. I had every confidence that once he was willing to do this, we would be set free from the abuse - once and for all.

I always believed that he was the husband God had given me, and together we would be victorious. I loved my husband in spite of everything, because God gave me a special love for him. I had confidence that the Lord would not let me down. He had come through for me time and time again. He would deliver.

CHAPTER FOUR
HOPE DEFERRED

Hope deferred makes the heart sick, but a longing fulfilled is a tree of life. Proverbs 13:12 (NIV)

It seemed to me that I prayed every possible prayer, confessed every possible scripture, cast every possible care, and fasted often. I anointed my house with oil and believed God for deliverance. It seemed as though the more I prayed, the worse things became. The abuse grew more intense, more violent, and more frequent.

You must understand, as a minister's wife there were not many people I could talk to about this problem. As a result, I kept it to myself. Even though we talked about the fact that he needed help, my husband went for counseling only after he thought I might leave him. After all, he had an image to maintain.

However, after a session or two, he made up one excuse after another as to the reason why he had to miss his next appointment. It was weeks before I discovered that he was no longer going for counseling.

Since that time, I've learned his behavior was, and is a typical pattern for abusive husbands. A cycle of promises to get help (as if to give recognition to the problem and a sense of hope), followed by excuses not to go for that help (thereby denying a problem exists or indicating an unwillingness to face it). In our case, even after I found a place that offered help in a private environment, a retreat setting designed especially for ministers with problems, he still refused to go.

We had two beautiful children. But because my husband had a spirit of violence which nothing seemed to control, they too were sometimes injured. In fact, the very first time he became violent was not long after we brought our new born son home after spending 3 months in the intensive care nursery. That particular evening, my husband came home from a meeting at the church and without warning, he started turning over furniture and throwing punches. From there, he went into the nursery, took our tiny son out of his crib, suspended him in mid-air and dropped him on his head.

The police refused to arrest him when they found out he was a minister. Thankfully, our son survived.

I knew that God knew my heart, and even though it seemed as if the more I prayed, the worse things became; I decided that I would do as I had done since childhood - confess exactly what I was feeling. How could God let something like this happen when He knew I had nowhere else to turn for help?

I walked by faith, read the Word, and witnessed to others, even after my husband no longer allowed me to participate in church activities. Besides being my husband, he was also my pastor and I had to honor his decisions in that regard. Still, my personal walk with the Lord was not shaken. My husband knew me well enough to know that I would continue to pray and trust God and he ridiculed me for this frequently.

> ***I will say unto God my rock, Why hast thou forgotten me? Why go I mourning because of the oppression of the enemy?***
>
> ***As with a sword in my bones, mine enemies reproach me; while they say daily unto me, where is thy God?***
> ***Psalms 42:9-10 (KJV)***

My only source of strength, my only hope was the Lord. And my husband was doing an excellent job of mocking that relationship. I never saw him so much as lose his temper with men, yet he would use all of his strength against me. Then, he would stand in my face and yell, "I know you're binding the devil right now, but it's not going to do you any good! I know you're praying, but God's not going to stop me or do anything to me! You're the one who's always sick!"

In actuality, he set before me the same challenge that King Nebuchadnezzar set before the three Hebrew boys before throwing them into the fiery furnace: *"What god will be able to rescue you from my hand?" (Daniel 3:15)*. In other words: where is your God?

It was unbelievable that this could be happening! How could he get up in the pulpit week after week, and preach as he did when he so boldly mocked God's authority at home?

Eventually, I began to wear down. It was distressing trying to hide scars and bruises. It was difficult not to make a sound when it hurt so badly to be hugged by people after church.

In exhaustion and frustration, I began questioning: Doesn't God honor faithfulness? Aren't we supposed to reap what we've sown? Wasn't God my champion, my refuge, my protector, and my defender? Why was this happening? Where was He? Had I been holding on to Him and His Word in vain? The children and I had done nothing to warrant this kind of treatment.

After all the hours of prayer, all the hope and confidence in the promises in God's Word, keeping everything to myself, taking care of the children, keeping up with the daily chores, and finally dealing with open humiliation and ridicule from my husband; I ultimately began to feel that God had abandoned and betrayed me.

I was filled with so many emotions. Hate, anger, hurt, frustration, and fear. Fear such as I'd never known before or since. I never thought that anything so awful could happen to me.

I had seen God's protection from harm when someone pulled a gun on me while doing street evangelism. The man was rendered helpless and (much to his surprise) was unable to pull the trigger. Why was I not protected from violence ***in my own home?***

I never expected to ever feel that I could not depend upon the Lord for the protection to which I had become accustomed. Then again, neither did I expect to be mistreated by my husband, the man who served the Lord with me.

> *If an enemy were insulting me, I could endure*
> *it; if a foe were rising against me, I could hide. But it was you, a man like myself, my companion, my close friend, with whom I once enjoyed sweet fellowship at the house of God, as we walked about among the worshippers*
> *Psalms 55:12-14 (NIV)*

I had reached the breaking point and had finally told the Lord about my anger, frustration, and the hatred in my heart. Hatred was an emotion I never imagined I would ever feel toward another human being. I blamed God for that, too. If He had intervened sooner, it would never have gotten to this point.

Yes, I was angry. But even more than that, I was so lonely and so very, very tired. It was suddenly so easy to give up. What was it all for anyway? God had turned His back on me. Of course, this is an old trick of the devil, to make a person feel isolated, alone, and overwhelmed. But, the knowledge of that did not change those feelings. I couldn't confess, fast, or pray those feelings away.

I shut the door on my relationship with the Lord and made an appointment at the beauty shop. Once there, I had my hair cut as short as possible. Cutting my hair was something I did not do. When my husband asked why, I told him I was in mourning for everything that had died in my life.

Along with my confessed hatred and anger, I was not speaking to God. For about two or three months, I was rather successful with this. Of course, that meant a drastic change in my lifestyle. I was the kind of person that kept a Bible at my bedside, because without reading the Word, I didn't have the strength to get out of bed in the morning. God was my life. I literally gained nourishment from His Word.

However, for the next several months, I forced myself to get out of bed; go to church; take care of the children; take care of the house; and generally, go through the motions. Since the violence would usually occur after a demonstration of certain gifts of the Spirit, (i.e., if I gave a word of knowledge to some-one which resulted in a praise report), I wanted no more of this business of being attacked in my own home *because I was living by the Word*. The situation appeared hopeless. I was through, finished, done with the whole thing!

Being angry with God didn't help matters. Things just grew worse. My husband began to verbally insult and try to belittle me in front of our associate ministers and church members. He continued to mock me because of illnesses which were often directly related to being kicked and beaten by him.

However, one day, while driving home, with the children asleep in the car, the Lord spoke to me very clearly. He said, "How can you say you love Me, Whom you have never seen, and hate your brother, whom you see every day?"

I responded, "I'm not speaking to you, Lord." But He asked me once again, "How can you say you love Me, Whom you have never seen, and hate your brother, whom you see every day?"

Once again, I said, "I'm not speaking to you, Lord." But He persisted and, a few moments later, once more He asked, "How can you say you love Me, Whom you have never seen, and hate your brother, whom you see every day?" By this time the words of 1 John 4:20 were rising up within me:

> *If anyone says, "I love God," yet hates his brother, he is a liar. For anyone who does not love his brother, whom he has seen, cannot love God whom he has not seen. And He has given us this command: Whoever loves God must also love his brother.*
> *1 John 4:20-21 (KJV)*

You see, although I had decided that I would not speak to the Lord again, I had never claimed to stop loving Him. I had never even considered the idea. I could not believe that the Lord was facing me with the issue of my love for Him at a time like this.

I began to pour out my heart to the Lord and express my anger and how unjustly I felt I was being treated. I slammed my hand down on the steering wheel and out poured all of the hurts, frustrations, and questions. Even though I could not, and still am not able to fully understand why things happened as they did; through time, the Lord has helped me to come to understand more and more.

Of course, I knew I had not made all the right choices while in the midst of that situation. I was not, and still am not, a flawless person. But, I was sure then and am still convinced that abuse is not God's will for **_anyone._**

As all of my anger came rushing out, it dawned on me that I was talking to the Lord. I had told Him everything that was in my heart before I realized that I had never expressed myself that way before - not to God. I mean, I was very, very angry about everything. However, when I got quiet, the strangest thing happened.

The Lord whispered in my right ear.

This time He said: "My shoulders are big enough to handle your anger." So, I continued to tell Him what was on my heart. The next thing He said was, "You MUST love him."

By this time, I was near my home and I surrendered. I said, "Lord, You know my heart, so I can't lie to you. I hate him, and You know I do, so I admit it. I know what Your Word says. If you want me to love him, You'll have to do it, because I can't. You'll have to teach me how to love him. You'll have to love him through me."

I did not realize that, in order to be able to allow God's love to flow through me, I had to come into a deeper understanding of His love. The Lord had been dealing with me about forgiveness throughout the course of this entire situation. I had often prayed over and over, "Lord, I forgive him, I forgive, in the name of Jesus," in obedience to the Word. Only, now that I understood that my love walk was in question, I felt that the matter of forgiveness was shaky, at best.

Needless to say, development of the "love department" required lots of time in prayer and in the Word. During this time, God began to place a genuine love in my heart for my husband - such as I'd never known before.

Little did I know, this was just the beginning of things to come. There was more that God desired to accomplish in me and now, my heart was in a position to receive. At the time, I did not understand it. At first, I didn't even notice it, but everyday while either reading the Word or praying, I saw something that I needed to work on - in myself.

Dear friends, let us love one another, for love

> *comes from God. Everyone who loves has been born of God and knows God.*
> *I John 4:7 (NIV)*

The anger in my heart was replaced with shock and amazement as I began to realize that I had never really loved my husband the way I should have in the first place. What I thought was love for my husband throughout our marriage was nothing at all compared to what God gave when I allowed Him to teach me how to love.

As I allowed God to pour His love out to my husband through me, once again, I realized that I really could do nothing without Him. It was not safe to trust my head, or my heart; but rather, in all my ways I had to acknowledge, know, and recognize Him (Proverbs 3:6).

As God's love began to operate in me, I asked Him to forgive me for being so childish. Then, I knew that I had to also forgive my husband. I didn't feel anything special. All I wanted was to obey the Word. I forgave my husband by faith, not by feeling.

It suddenly seemed so foolish to feel that God was not interested in what happened to me. My heart had been wrong. My attitude had been wrong. I wasn't even walking in love, the very basic and most vital element of the Christian life. The Word of God said I had been living a lie.

All I could think about for the next few weeks was the fact that there was such a change needed in me, while all this time I had been praying for a change in my husband.

> *Why do you look at the (insignificant) speck that is in your brother's eye, but do not notice and acknowledge the (egregious) log that is*

> *in your own eye? Or, how can you say to your brother, 'Let me get the speck out of your eye,' when there is a log in your own eye? You hypocrite, (play-actor, pretender), first get the log out of your own eye, (remove unforgiveness from your heart) and then you will see clearly to take the speck out of your brother's eye*
> *Matthew 7:3-5 (AMP)*

There was simply a wonderful difference in me and the way I expressed my love for my husband. God's love was pouring out from me through the power of His precious Holy Spirit (Romans 5:5), and my relationship with Him had been restored.

> *But when He, the Spirit of truth comes, He will guide you into all truth.... John 16:13a (NIV)*

Just as He had dealt with me about love and forgiveness, the Lord also began to shine His light on other areas of my life as well. Every time I picked up my Bible, I found something else that spoke to me so clearly, that I could not rest until I began to work on that area in light of the Word. Although I was very concerned about the abusive situation, God seemed more concerned that I walk right before Him.

Working on those areas of my life required me to be willing to change. As I saw attitudes or conduct that did not line up with the Word of God, I pressed in and made the necessary corrections. This was not an easy process. I had to be willing to allow the Holy Spirit to take me out of my comfort zone and shine His light into the private chambers of my heart.

It was hard to come face to face with the reality of the need to shake off old habits, thoughts, and behaviors at a time when I felt more important things were going wrong in my life. To be honest, I was dealing with an "I'm a good Christian" mentality.

The first three things the Lord dealt with me about were love, forgiveness, and bitterness. After that, He began to take me through each of the fruit of the Spirit: joy, peace, long-suffering, gentleness, goodness, faith, meekness, temperance (Galatians 5:22-23).

While researching each subject, I began taking away from and adding to my thoughts and conduct according to the principles I was learning. It amazed me how God could be changing me so much in the middle of such a stressful time in my life.

My relationship with the Lord became very intimate. Even though I was not sure just what He was doing about my marriage; I had no doubt that He would heal, deliver, and restore.

No, my husband had not changed. The circumstances had not changed, but I had changed.

CHAPTER FIVE
YOU MUST FORGIVE

But if you do not forgive, neither will your Father, who is in heaven, forgive your sins.
Mark 11:26 (KJV)

As previously stated, the Lord had been dealing with me about forgiveness throughout the course of this experience. One morning, during my prayer time, He very distinctly told me that I had to ask my husband to forgive me for the animosity I had held in my heart against him.

I COULD NOT BELIEVE IT!!

Not after all I'd been through! Yes, I was changed. The Lord had done a definite work in my heart, but the abuse had not stopped. After struggling with it for a few days, I concluded that all I could do was obey. The only way I had made it this far was by leaning on the Lord. It only made sense to continue trusting Him, even now.

The anticipation of this encounter began to cause hope to rise up within me. It was all worked out in my mind just how things would happen. To begin with, I would tell my husband how much stronger and deeper my love was for him. Then, I would tell him what a difference the Lord had made in me. Lastly, there would be a wonderful reconciliation and all would be well. I was already looking forward to the day when we could both give testimony to all that we had been through, and of our victory in Jesus.

Finally, the stage was set. My husband had come home one afternoon and did not appear to be in a hurry to leave. While sitting in our den, I nervously prayed under my breath, not wishing to make the mistake of putting off what I knew I must do for the wrong reasons. It would have been so easy to continually question the timing and my husband's possible temperament, and use that as my excuse to be disobedient about what the Lord told me I must do.

Consequently, I began my speech - watching his face intently. When I finished, he began to curse me and left the house. This was not the outcome I had envisioned. I began to wonder why I had to go through all of this.

For the next several months, my husband spent all of his days on the job of another woman who was also a member of our church. Our home was next door to the church and she lived three doors away. Our family car remained in her driveway all night. He would bring home his dirty clothes and pick up clean ones. Sometimes we saw him, sometimes we did not.

He boldly began to see this woman, as well as other women from our church. The deacons and the church board did not seem to care. Even when he openly dated some of their relatives, nothing was said about removing him from his position. When I did see him, he laughed as he reminded me that the church would never get rid of him.

Six months prior, he had convinced me that he needed my help and support in the ministry. I had been working for a short time, with his consent, mainly because we needed furniture. During that time, I had started savings accounts for us at our bank, and individual accounts for the children at the credit union at my job.

I believed him when he said he needed more of my help and support with the ministry. I responded to his request and quit my job.

But one day, shortly after he had stopped coming home, I was notified by the bank that our savings accounts had been closed. Also, the credit union alerted me that almost all of the children's savings had been withdrawn as well.

The Lord continued focusing my attention on areas of my life that were out of line with His Word and His will. I'll admit that at the time, I did not fully understand this, but I loved Jesus, and wanted to obey Him. Quite naturally, my priority was the abuse, in other words, my relationship with my husband. But God's priority was my relationship with Him.

> **"For my thoughts are not your thoughts, neither are your ways my ways." declares the Lord.**
> **"As the heavens are higher than the earth, so are my ways higher than your ways and my thoughts higher than your thoughts."**
> **Isaiah 55:8-9 (AMP)**

The turning point came when I discovered that I was pregnant. I must admit that I had mixed emotions about the pregnancy. I remember wishing the circumstances in our home were different. I wasn't sure how or when I should tell my husband. For that matter, I wasn't even sure if I should tell him at all. Since he no longer lived in our home, I seldom saw him. Sometimes I found his dirty clothes on the floor in our bedroom and wondered when he had come and gone.

At one time, we had wanted a daughter, but I also wanted it to be a joyous time in our lives; a time without the darkness and the spirit of violence that had settled over our home. I never knew for sure just how my husband felt about the pregnancy; the news didn't change anything. He still didn't come home, the little money I had was running out, and I began to wonder how much longer I could afford to go without seeking medical attention.

I had stopped going to the church. I could no longer stand to hear him say how much he loved me from the pulpit, while we both knew of the brutality he was inflicting in our home. He had even stopped wearing his wedding band, which I found on the desk in our room one day after he had dropped off his dirty clothes.

I continued to prepare dinner every day as if he were coming home to be with the family. The children didn't seem to notice anything out of the ordinary.

One Sunday evening, he came home after church, and as he began to go through the pots, I asked him for the keys to the car. It was dark out and I needed to go to the corner grocer to get milk for the children. He questioned me, but gave me the keys.

I felt uneasy as I went to the door, but thought it was just my imagination. Every-thing would be alright. After all, I was just going to the store.

As I was getting into the car, I suddenly felt the car door close, crushing me. I thought quickly, "If I give him the keys and ask him to go pick up the milk instead, he'll back off and leave me alone." But there was a rage erupting inside of him from which there was no escape. There was no reasoning or getting away from him.

I gave him the keys, ran to the house, and noticed that he quickly followed. Over and over I reminded him that I was nearly five months pregnant. That made no difference. The children were in the room screaming and crying. That made no difference. He continued to punch, kick, and throw me into the wall.

"I know you're binding the devil," he kept repeating. "That's not going to work against me."

There was broken glass on the floor from the vases I had thrown at him, in my defense, which cut deep gashes into the soles of my feet. I couldn't get the children out of the room. I wasn't sure if he would hurt them or if he were only after me. The last time I was slammed against the wall, I realized I was going to lose the baby.

As I slid to the floor, I watched him look down at me with what seemed to be contempt. I told him that I needed to get to a hospital, and that I was losing the baby. He simply ran out the door, jumped into the car, and drove away.

I crawled through the den and down the long hall to the bedroom. The children were screaming and crying, but I didn't have the strength to even pick myself up. My head was swimming. I knew I losing consciousness. I didn't want the children to see this.

It seemed to be only a short time after I closed the door to my room, that I heard someone in the house calling my name, looking for me. I soon recognized the voice to be the 18 year old son of one of the members of our church who lived next door. He had been taking a short-cut through the joint parking lot between the church and parsonage on his way home. When he noticed our door was open and heard the children crying, he came in to investigate.

He knocked on my bedroom door and asked if he should go get his mom or call an ambulance. Horrified and embarrassed, I rejected his offer. He then cleaned up my children and put them to bed. He also cleaned up the glass and blood in the den and left. How humiliating to be assisted at a time like this by one of the young people at our church.

No, I didn't want an ambulance or any outsiders in my home. What would I say? How could I tell anyone, least of all total strangers, that my husband and pastor had left me to bleed to death in front of our children? There would be lights and police in front of the church parsonage - and this was such a gossiping little town. They would never let the children and I have any peace. There would be questions and whispers and probing for explanations. How do you explain a violent, cruel, and abusive pastor, husband, and father?

As I lost consciousness across my bed, through my mind ran the hardest question of all: where was God?

CHAPTER SIX
PRAY, PRAY, PRAY

The next morning, one of our associate ministers and his wife (my prayer partner) were in prayer when she said she heard the Spirit speak my name and the word "miscarriage". They rushed to my home and took me for medical treatment. My physician informed me that it was a miracle that I was still alive. He said I should have bled to death during the night.

The plain truth is, there are 3-4 million women and children each year affected by abuse in this country. The stories are as varied as there are women. The sad part of my experience was how many ministers, deacons, elders, and other ministry leader-ship wives confided in me about their abusive marriages while I was a pastor's wife. They turned to me, from various denominations, for prayer and support - never realizing that I was going through a nightmare of my own. I had felt so alone. Surely this could not be happening to other Christians, especially those in ministry leadership.

But, I was wrong.

I would listen in shock as these women expressed and described identical feelings which I also felt. The hurt, the total outrage, the concern for their children, the confusion, the humiliation in front of others, hiding scars and bruises, trying to "carry on as usual" in their roles within the church, and always, always… the hours in prayer.

I can never express how very important prayer is in the life of a believer. The most touching experience that was shared with me was that of a widow in her 70's. She was in the audience the first time I shared my testimony on television. We went to lunch together afterwards and I listened as she talked about the strength she had gained from spending hours a day in prayer throughout her marriage to an abusive pastor. Her daughter was with her and she shared how her own faith in God remained strong, in spite of the abuse, because she was able to observe her mother's consistent communion with God during the worst time of their lives.

And hours in prayer is what my prayer partner and I spent every morning over the next several weeks. For the first time, I was able talk with someone about the ordeal the children and I had been facing for the last several years. She listened and prayed with me.

The previous year, my husband and I had agreed to separate for a short time to fast and pray, and to allow the Lord to do a work in us to bring about a healing in our marriage. But the separation following the miscarriage had no prior discussion. I had grown progressively weaker after the miscarriage, and without food or money to feed the children, I finally contacted my father for a loan. He volunteered to pick up the children instead.

He worked in the same city and had heard the rumors. Although he respected the fact that I was praying for God to work a miracle, as He had done so many times before in our lives. Naturally, he wanted the children in a safer environment.

When he arrived to pick up the children, I realized that without food or money, I was not going to get any better. I got into the car with them. My husband had not been home for so long, I've often wondered when he actually realized we were gone.

CHAPTER SEVEN
STRANGE ATTRACTIONS

We had married while we were both in college, pursuing what God had called each of us to do. I had not completed my B.S.N. (Bachelor of Science in Nursing) degree at the time, but now a door had been opened for me to attend a Licensed Vocational Nursing (LVN) program at a local junior college.

Even though I knew the Lord had called me to be an RN, this one year program would be free (scholarship), so I started school. To be perfectly honest, when I considered the fact that I was now alone with two children, I just didn't have the faith to believe that the Lord would sustain us through the two to three years I would need to complete an RN (BSN) degree.

That time in school was not an easy time. In fact, it took all that was in me to keep going each day. People approached me with gossip and off-colored comments about the scandal that surrounded our separation. Some would confront me in the supermarket to tell me I was crazy to leave "such a Godly man."

I moved to a nearby town. My phone number and place of residency was kept secret to avoid harassment and any possible physical danger. However, acting on legal advice, I eventually provided my husband with the information necessary to contact me in order to allow him the opportunity to arrange to see the children. I realized that was a mistake when, only one hour after I had given him our address and unlisted phone number, I received my first phone call and "visit" from one of the women he had been seeing.

Every time I changed to a new unlisted number, the phone calls began again, always a short time after he had been given the information. Women would continually call to harass, curse, and even to ask me if I was sure the marriage was over so that they could pursue my husband. His girlfriends would show up at my apartment. Most of them actually told me that they would soon be taking my place as the pastor's wife. It concerned me that these women were obviously getting their information about how to contact me from none other than my husband himself, even though he denied it.

This foolish behavior never ceased to amaze me. After all, these women were not strangers. I knew them very well. All of them were members of our church.

For various reasons, some women seem to have a tendency to be attracted to men in the forefront or in leadership. Some athletes, politicians, musicians, actors, etc., have bragged that women in large numbers are willing to do almost anything to be with them. Many times, these men admit to not receiving very much attention from women at all before they became well known.

Ministry positions, including the pastoral office, are a position of leadership that is also attractive to women. Several years ago, I attended a Christian singles' conference where I was literally shocked at the number of women who so openly thrust themselves upon the minister in charge. It was very disappointing to see that their behavior was not discouraged by him. Don't misunderstand, I <u>firmly</u> believe that it is the responsibility of both the Christian man AND woman to live a life that is well pleasing to the Lord.

My husband and I were approached by women in the church who stated that they believed God had shown them that I would soon die and they had already been chosen to be his next wife. This is apparently such a common occurrence that I have heard the same account from almost every pastor and wife I've met. All of our pastor friends talked about how often they were approached by women with lustful desires.

During counseling sessions, it was very common for me to hear women express their unhappiness over the fact that their husbands didn't do or say certain things in the same fashion as the pastor or some other man in the church administration. Many of us talk to women everyday in our churches who express similar feelings.

It would take another book to attempt to explain why so many women seek attention from, and are willing to do almost anything to be with men of prominence, but it happens.

The fact is, these women have either put that person on an extremely high pedestal, or they're living in a fantasy world. Either way, they can be easily seduced, manipulated, and taken advantage of by the man that is the object of their interest. When a man, who is in ministry, (or any other form of leadership), takes advantage of their role or position in order to sleep with these women, that is also abuse - even if the woman involved is a consenting party.

It was about two years after my husband had left us that I learned his adulterous affairs with women in the church had actually begun within months after he became the pastor. It was sobering to realize that the abuse going on in our home extended to the congregation. They were also victims.

When we first assumed the position as pastor and wife, an "Installation Service" was held, at which time, our pastor gave several strict charges to both my husband and myself. One of the charges given to my husband was: if anything were to happen to me (meaning death), while he was still the pastor, and he had a desire to remarry, he was not to consider looking among the flock that he pastored. Our pastor went on to say, that even the hint of "dating among the congregation" would cause conflict, distraction, competition, and hurt feelings; which would in turn hinder the effectiveness of the ministry.

He was telling us that a valuable bond of trust, so vital to the relationship between a pastor and his congregation, is violated by romantic involvement.

The standards Christian men and women are to live by should not be defined by headlines when they are so clearly delineated in the Word of God. Recent headlines demonstrate how the integrity of the minister, as well as the ministry can so easily be called into question.

CHAPTER EIGHT
SPIRIT-FILLED COUNSEL

I continued to pray that God would restore our marriage. After all, I was certain that this was the man God had ordained to be my husband. Jesus said that He is the giver of abundant life, while satan's goal is only to kill, steal, and destroy (John 10:10). There was no way I could allow the enemy to destroy our family and steal our future.

Finally, one day, my husband began talking about reconciliation. He said I was the only wife the Lord had given him and he was not willing to lose his family. I felt sure that God was answering my prayers, but I had to be firm and hold my ground about certain things. For example, I refused to allow him to merely spend the night with me occasionally - as he desired to do. I was his wife, not his mistress, and refused to be treated as such.

I was astounded when my husband agreed to Christian marriage counseling with a Spirit-filled minister. This was something he had always opposed because he insisted that I had already spoken with these ministers about what was happening. He was sure that they were all prejudiced against him.

Of course, he knew this was not true. The one thing he always said he was grateful for was my silence.

We had only spoken to one minister in the past, who was not very much help. In fact, this particular minister had told me, (in the presence of my husband), that my husband may have justification to hit me if I continued to refuse to have sex with him immediately after he beat me up, since that's what he enjoyed. (Needless to say, I never wanted to "counsel" with this man again).

At this time; however, my husband was expressing a desire for counseling and picked a pastor that he felt neither one of us knew. We made the appointment, and as I was praying in preparation, the Lord spoke to me and told me not to say a word throughout the session. I was not sure how that would be possible. We had conducted marriage counseling sessions ourselves. The pastor was sure to ask us both questions, and he would expect us both to answer.

I liked this pastor and his wife from the moment we first met. The pastor explained to us that he always conducted counseling sessions with his wife present. We opened with prayer and I felt the sweet presence of God fill the room. I was at peace that the Lord was going to make it possible for me to be obedient to His instructions.

It was difficult for me not to show any emotion as the conversation progressed. My husband dominated the conversation. I listened in shock as he made it sound as if our problems were simply the stress of doing the Lord's work in the midst of problems that were common experiences of any pastor of any church, anywhere. He explained that the stress was compounded by the struggle of being a young pastor.

There were members who had a history of practicing witchcraft - a practice they wished to continue, coupled with their traditional denominational background which often rose up in opposition to his sermons on living in obedience to the Spirit.

He was telling the truth about those problems, but the abuse, the very reason we were separated, was never mentioned.

Finally, the pastor leaned forward and looked my husband straight in the eye and asked him if he had ever hit or abused me in any fashion. My husband said no - even after being asked several times. I kept praying within myself and wondering how he could be so comfortable telling these lies. How could he expect me to believe that he was serious about saving our marriage?

The session finally ended and we stood and joined hands for a closing prayer. As the pastor prayed he suddenly looked up at my husband and asked him why he had lied. He then went on to share what God had revealed to him. I never had to say a word.

Everything my husband had done to me was revealed to this pastor by the Holy Spirit. He couldn't accuse me of telling this pastor anything in advance.

I began to praise the Lord. This was the reason I had desired counseling with someone who was Spirit-filled and Spirit-led. I thought about Ananias and Sapphira in the book of Acts chapter 5. They lied to Peter, but the Holy Spirit revealed the lies immediately. God had fought the battle for me. The Lord had been my defender and advocate.

My husband cried and admitted that he had lied. The pastor went on to say, by revelation, that my husband had slept with so many women in the congregation and had done so much damage, that he needed to give up his role as pastor, move away, and let the Lord bring in a pastor that was really going to help the people. My husband admitted that this was the same thing the Lord had been saying to both of us for several months.

We left the office together and went to the parsonage. For the first time we talked openly and freely about the problem for several hours. We agreed that our personal problems were destroying us as well as hindering us from doing the work God had called us to do.

The Lord had told us from the beginning, we were only to be at that church for seven years. After seven years, we were to move to Dallas, Texas and begin a new phase of ministry. As the violence progressed, we had discussed the fact that the Lord wanted us to move on, get alone with Him, and allow Him to bring deliverance and restoration; but my husband was never willing to leave. That evening, he decided that it was best for all concerned to be obedient to the Spirit of God. We decided to start over together.

The next morning, I went to school, leaving the children at the parsonage with him. However, things were very different when I returned. My husband confronted me in the den and accused me of trying to "trick" him into giving up the church. He went on to say that if I wanted to stay married to him there would be no more Christian marriage counseling. He also said that I could not read my Bible, watch Christian television, or pray in the house - at least not while he was there.

Further stipulations were: his girl friends would be able to come over whenever they wished and if I didn't like it, I was to go back in the bedroom and stay during their visits.

Lastly, he stated that if I wanted a Christian marriage or relationship, then I didn't want him. I told him that he could not control my prayer life and my personal time with the Lord.

"Like I said, if you want that Christian stuff you don't want me," he said.

I began to wonder what he would do to try and stop me. It occurred to me that the women he had been involved with seemed to be willing to compromise all Christian values in order to see him. For some reason, I asked him if he felt that women wanted him so much that they were willing to do anything to be with him?

He smirked. I suppose he knew that I was not one of those women.

I thought to myself, "Maybe that was why he was so violent toward me. Maybe he was trying to break me, to control me in some way."

When I told him that his demands were impossible because it would mean that I would have to give up my personal relationship with the Lord in order to have a relationship with him, he insisted that I had to submit to his wishes or forget the marriage. I asked him if he really knew what he was saying, and pleaded with him to reconsider. He would not.

I finally said, "I accepted Christ when I was nine years old. I knew the Lord before I knew your name, even before I knew you existed. I will not give up my Lord or my relationship with Him for you."

It wasn't until the children and I reached the apartment that I realized it was over. It didn't seem real. I could not believe that he was actually going to continue to pastor after he had tried to get me to denounce the very faith that he preached about each and every week. He had destroyed my trust, destroyed our relationship, and now he had attempted to destroy my personal relationship with the Lord.

I looked around my apartment with very little furniture, few dishes, and two children, (ages two and three), and realized that on that afternoon, in the den of my home, not on foreign soil as I had always imagined, I had given up what I knew to be everything for Christ.

CHAPTER NINE
PERSECUTED FOR HIS NAME

Strengthening the disciples and encouraging them to remain true to the faith, "We must go through many hardships to enter the kingdom of God," they said. Acts 14:22 (NIV)

Perhaps one of the reasons it's so hard for us, as believers in Christ, to accept experiences such as mine is because whenever we think of tragic things happening in the lives of Christians, it's so easy **not** to think. It is easy to forget that there are many reasons why difficult times enter our lives. It's too convenient to place the blame on the doorstep of: lack of faith, bad confessions, and wrong teaching.

Suffering and abuse does not always occur because you have done something wrong. In actuality, the Bible teaches that there are other reasons, as well. Jesus was constantly persecuted by religious people, and finally put to death, yet

He had done no wrong.

Mark 4:17 says persecution can come into our lives because of the Word of God. In fact, 2 Timothy 3:12 says, *"Everyone who wants to live a Godly life in Christ Jesus will be persecuted."*

We see the miracles of the apostles, and too often we *think* we want to live in the book of the Acts. We see supernatural deliverance from prisons, great acts of faith, angelic manifestations, and the apostles taking authority over spirits as they took and shook entire cities for God. They had a reputation as being the people who turned their world upside down (Act 17:6).

While we get caught up in what we read about their experiences, as exciting as they were, too often, we do not recognize the facts. In this same book of Acts, Stephen was falsely accused and then stoned to death **AS HE WAS PREACHING THE GOSPEL.** James was beheaded. Paul was beaten many times, shipwrecked three times, stoned, and left for dead.

Although Paul was compelled by the Holy Spirit to go to Jerusalem, he was also warned by the Spirit that persecution and imprisonment awaited him (Acts 20). In the same book of Acts, even though Peter was released from prison supernaturally, he was still beaten, as were Paul and Silas. In fact, most of the apostles were eventually martyred for their faith in God.

Many people say that we need to live like the people lived in the Bible. Well, read your Bible. Great victories were often preceded by a period of great pain and suffering.

Abuse cases are very individual. In my case, the abuse was most often linked to anything associated with my relationship with the Lord: operating in the gifts, obeying the call of God upon my life, or simply something I had said or done in reference to the Bible. Even though I had read the Bible and fully understood that the apostles (and Christ Himself) were also persecuted because of Godly living, it did not occur to me to draw that conclusion in my own situation. As stated earlier, ***"everyone who wants to live a Godly life in Christ Jesus will be persecuted" (2 Timothy 3:12).***

The conclusion I had drawn was that I must love God, no matter what it cost me, not realizing that loving God and living a Godly life are synonymous, the same thing. They must walk hand-in-hand. And that's exactly what the apostles were doing in the book of Acts. They loved God enough to continue to live for Him, no matter what the cost.

This was not a new concept either for the apostles or myself. Such was the case with the three Hebrew boys Shadrach, Meshach, and Abed-nego when they were given the choice of worshiping the image of the king or remaining true worshipers of God:

> ***Shadrach, Meshach, and Abed-nego replied to the king, "O Nebuchadnezzar, we do not need to defend ourselves before you in this matter.***
>
> ***If we are thrown into the blazing furnace, the***
> ***God we serve is able to save us from it, and He will rescue us from your hand, O king.***
>
> ***BUT EVEN IF HE DOES NOT, we want you to know, O king, that we will not serve your gods or worship the image of gold you have set up." Daniel 3:16-18 (NIV)***

God brought them through their situation. They had confidence in God's ability to deliver. Yet, they were fully prepared to be cast into the furnace, even if the Lord had not delivered.

> ***BUT EVEN IF HE DOES NOT, we want you to know, O king, that we will not serve your gods or worship the image of gold you you have set up." Daniel 3:18***

Keep this in mind, the next time you're wondering why something devastating, such as abuse has occurred in the life of a fellow believer. Don't be so quick to condemn them. If you believe that Christians never suffer, obviously the Word demonstrates something other than what you believe.

Believing that bad things never happen to Christians can be a contributing factor to why women who are alone as a result of an abusive, rebellious husband are put out of some churches. The fact that their lives were in danger, that the husband was not repentant, or even that she had been abandoned does not matter.

In my case, I was asked to leave a church, but MY HUSBAND was the one who had rebelled against the things of God and walked out on us. I was cast aside because I was the victim of someone else's wrong-doing. It is wrong for someone who has suffered the nightmare of abuse to suffer further abuse in the form of rejection by other church 'leaders'.

The National Domestic Violence Hotline
1-800-799-7233 OR 1-800-787-3224 (TTY)

SECTION TWO
INTRODUCTION

Through conversations with other abused women who are (or have been) married to someone in ministry leadership, I discovered that we were so much alike. We had similar questions and issues in common, only a few of which I will address in this section. If you are a reader who knows someone who has been in this situation, perhaps an understanding of what they may be going through, both spiritually and emotionally can help you be a more understanding and supportive friend or advisor.

The National Domestic Violence Hotline
1-800-799-7233 OR 1-800-787-3224 (TTY)

CHAPTER TEN
SOMEONE TO CONFIDE IN

The feelings of isolation, and lack of an outlet experienced by abused women is a common tactic of the enemy. Christian women in abusive situations often have the perception that there is no help available, coupled with a fear that no one will believe them. And if she is believed, she faces the possibility of dealing with the humiliation of public exposure and of rejection. The combination of these fears can cause them to feel isolated and left alone to deal with a volatile situation.

This occurs because many times, as in my case, friends that are also confidants for ministers and their wives can be very limited. Frequently, immediate friends are members of the congregation, members of the ministry staff, or ministers from other churches. It can be difficult to judge who to trust with such a confidence.

One day, one of the ministers at our church witnessed an attack on me by my husband in our home. From then on he treated me with anger, and accused me of trying to destroy my husband's ministry. He felt that if the congregation knew that the pastor was capable of such brutality, they would terminate his position. But for some reason, he blamed me for his pastor's behavior. Several years after our divorce this minister apologized to me for his attitude and actions toward me.

This is but one example of the kind of experience which can make someone hesitate to consider seeking help or counseling. Of course, I did not know it at the time, but it is common for men to blame the woman for the actions of the abuser. This kind of thinking is in the world, but can be found in the church, as well.

It can be very dangerous for an abused woman to confide in someone she thinks she can trust, only to find later that the person has revealed their conversation to her husband. Sometimes the person in whom she confided may think they are being helpful; but unless they are truly led by the Spirit of God, they usually open the door for the abuser to have another excuse to vent his rage. She is then left alone to face the consequences of someone else's bad judgement.

Another reason why it can be difficult for a woman to find someone to turn to is the self-righteousness of others. Friends can suddenly become so self-righteous, beating a believer over the head with accusations of lack of faith, or not walking in the Spirit. They usually do not understand that this woman has probably been holding on to the Lord with all she's got, usually for quite some time, ***long*** before they were aware that there was even a problem. Her self-esteem may be very low. She may be on the verge of giving up on herself. She may be in an emotional state of mind that will not take much of that kind of badgering. She may be close to going over the edge, and possibly close to abdicating what faith in God she's got left.

Many times believers make these comments without praying. Notice I said without "praying". I did not say without "thinking". We say some of the things we say because we **are** thinking. Keep in mind that the Word says, in Proverbs 3:6, *"In all your ways acknowledge Him (God), and He will direct your path."* My personal definition of wisdom is: knowing when to speak the words of God, and instead of your own opinion.

> ***"For My thoughts are not your thoughts,***
> ***neither are your ways My ways,"***
> ***declares the Lord.***
>
> *As the heavens are higher than*
> *the earth, so are My ways higher than your*
> *ways and My thoughts than your thoughts.*
> *Isaiah 55:8-9 (KJV)*

How many times have we felt it was alright to do or say a certain something, only to find out that even though *we* felt it was the right thing, it wasn't what God wanted at all. The Holy Spirit is such a Gentleman and He knows how to make us sensitive to such things.

Saying things without praying includes such comments as: "Don't worry, everything is alright." No. Everything is *not* alright. Other such comments are: "you don't have enough faith," or "you need strength to go through," or "I know Brother (or Sister) So and So, he (or she) would never do anything to hurt you."

Obviously, also not true. It's easy to say nice things. It takes the wisdom of God to say the right thing, or even nothing at all. It's not always necessary to say anything. These are the times that praying in tongues with someone can be so valuable.

Another thing we should keep in mind is that at any given time, we are all on different planes and pursuing our own personal agendas with the Lord. For example, the Lord may be dealing with a brother about walking in forgiveness. That brother will be searching the Word, studying, and doing research about forgiveness. Almost every time you see him, his conversation will somehow be turned in the direction of forgiveness.

You know how it is when the Spirit is dealing with you about something. Everything you read, hear, or see will seem to be related to whatever it is the Lord is dealing with you about. Consequently, when given the opportunity to talk to a believer about a problem in their life, that particular subject is so prevalent in your mind until that is what you will minister. Not because it is what that sister or brother needs, but rather, that is what is dominant in your spirit at the time. You may even feel that the Holy Spirit "told" you to say that, when in actuality, it was your own human spirit.

The final point in this chapter is perhaps the most obvious if the abuser is in ministry leadership. Many times these men are surrounded by people who have put them on such a pedestal, that the wife can very easily feel that no one will believe her. It can be painful to have members of the church community accusing her of being a liar. Many times even family members will not believe the abused spouse.

When one of the members of my own family found out the circumstances of my divorce, she informed me that she did not believe me. She said that she had called my former husband, and he denied the abuse - just as he had done with that pastor during marital counseling. I don't know any abuser that will shout that kind of information from the house tops. I was not surprised that he denied it, but I was surprised that she was so willing to believe him.

I thank God for that pastor and his wife who allowed the Holy Spirit to reveal the truth when they met with us. We must admit, there are some people who would rather believe anything else other than the truth when it comes to ministry leadership, whether it be good or bad.

I encourage those of you who may feel alone. God understands that you need a listening ear. He knows that you feel you have stood alone for so long, that you're about to give up. He is able to provide someone with both the wisdom and the understanding you need.

CHAPTER ELEVEN
A SPIRIT OF REJECTION

The children and I began attending a Charismatic church shortly after my marriage ended; but after about two years, I started to wonder if I'd made a mistake. People were leaving my husband's church and attending the church where we were. One lady in particular brought with her what was supposed to be "inside information" about my marriage, ministry, and divorce.

What she'd actually brought were gossip, rumors, and speculation about my personal life. She transferred to the same hospital at which the head elders of the church were employed and began working with his wife. They became close. I felt uncomfortable in my spirit, but did not know how extensive the situation had become until I started getting *special attention* during intercessory prayer services. (This was a weekly Bible study conducted by the head elders at the church.)

The elder's wife frequently had "a word" for me that was always condemning and accusatory. I soon stopped attending those meetings. But, one night, she stopped me on the steps in front of the church. Grabbing my arm, she accused me of being rebellious and angry with God.

"I saw you in a vision shaking your fist at God," she said. She insisted that I repent right then or something terrible would happen to me. Obviously, she had no idea how much the Lord had been dealing with me, calling me to walk pleasing before Him in order to survive the nightmare I had just been through and it's lingering effects. She had no idea of what it had cost me to remain faithful and obedient under the circumstances. In other words, she really didn't know what she was talking about. All she was doing was an excellent job of crushing my fragile heart and spirit. When I wouldn't "admit" what she wanted to hear, she became very angry.

However, God was faithful. I was about to leave the church when my pastor told me to make an appointment to see him that week. The Lord had shown him and his wife the truth about the situation, including the involvement of the young woman from my old church. My pastors knew what I had been through and wanted no more injury to be inflicted upon me.

The Lord had also shown them that the elders had been influenced because of the confidence they had in this woman. They gave me several options, but I elected to leave the situation in their hands. My pastors confronted the three of them in a private meeting.

After discussing that situation, my pastor began to teach me about the spirit of rejection and how it had entered my life through the abuse and subsequent divorce. He explained that the circumstances surrounding my divorce could cause a woman to began to ask questions that can compound the feelings of rejection. The questions he mentioned were the very ones I had been asking.

I wondered why the man I loved so much was so willing to mistreat and then abandon his family in exchange for his affairs. I had ask myself what was wrong with me as a woman? What could I have done differently? Once I found out the character of the type of women with whom he was involved, I wondered why being a Godly woman wasn't enough for a husband who preached Godliness and holiness?

My pastor seemed to bring up all the questions in my heart. He explained that if I didn't take authority over that spirit now, it would plague me for the rest of my life. He knew of my plan to leave the church because the spirit of rejection was already in operation. Therefore, it was able to manifest in various ways, as in the case with the two elders. The door was opened through the abuse and was "following" me.

"You may leave if you wish," he told me, "but you will probably continue to feel rejected on the job, in the church, or anywhere else you may go."

We prayed together and took authority over the spirit of rejection. They instructed me further on how to remain free, as well as signs and symptoms to watch for that would be an indication of that stronghold attempting to come against me again.

It is important to understand how easy it can be for the spirit of rejection to affect someone's life once the door has been opened. In my own life, even though God had miraculously spared my life and delivered me out of an abusive situation, it was as if little bits of arsenic had been deposited within me. Every aspect of my personality had been touched by that horrible experience and small portions of every aspect of my life had been eaten away.

As long as I was active, it kept me in a state of continually seeking the Lord's face, and He was always dealing with me. However, we moved to another town where I did occasional volunteer work in the nursery and in children's church. But the pastor advised me to sit still, because he felt I needed a season to "just receive healing."

I took his advice, but that did not work for me. Doing nothing only served to make me feel useless. Without the opportunity to even be a "doorkeeper in the house of God," the little confidence I had left in myself soon converted to weakened confidence in God. I no longer operated in the gift of miracles. My walk with God deteriorated. I put myself on a shelf.

As much as I would like to boast of remaining steadfast and unwavering - that would simply be untrue. Even though he had mistreated and abandoned us, my husband continued to pastor and go on with life and ministry, while I was the one who was being punished.

Everywhere we sought fellowship, the news of the divorce or the scandal surrounding it preceded us. For several years after receiving that bit of advice, I felt like a castaway, an unnecessary member of the body of Christ. My relationship with God was up and down and full of backsliding.

Perhaps this type of situation is the reason why I've met so many abused women, including former ministers' wives, who are completely backslidden. The spirit of rejection can be so overwhelming, that it can be easy to forget that the Word of God remains the same. He has promised to never leave you or forsake you. If you are plagued by a spirit of rejection in your life, God did not put it there; you've allowed it to remain. Sometimes just hearing a statement like this can arouse more feelings of rejection.

You may say that you've been through enough already. That's understandable, especially in light of the fact that, in addition to the rejection of a spouse, you may also be facing the possibility of rejection by friends or family, and maybe even your church, in some cases.

So, even though the rejection was not caused by you, you are the one that has to deal with it. Remember, you're the one making the choice to keep going (or, to get going again) in God. In order to do that, you have to be willing to go through the process necessary for your restoration and growth.

I often asked, why do I have to work so hard all the time? Such is life in the Spirit. If you desire to go on to victorious living in God, in spite of what you've been through, you'll have to be willing to work for your own deliverance. Realize the spirit of rejection will try to resurface in various ways, and you'll have to do battle against it.

Abuse, coupled with feelings of rejection are strategies of the enemy designed to make you feel like giving up on everything. At times, it is easier to give up than it is to be obedient to the will of God. But, in making the choice to go on with God, you have chosen life, because you have chosen to obey. In fact, Jesus said:

> ***Whoever has My commands and obeys them, he is the one who loves Me. He who loves Me will be loved by My Father, and I too will love him and show Myself to him.***
> ***John 14:21 (NIV)***

God does seem to expect more of you. But that's the way it usually is on the road to spiritual maturity. The more the enemy tries to steal from you, the more the Spirit of grace says, "to meet this challenge in your life, this is what you must add to your character and this is what you must take off." And as you obey His instructions, God will be faithful to guide you to a higher place in Him that you never would have known in your own will.

God often reassures me that He has never rejected me. I was finally set completely free from that nagging spirit of rejection when God gave me this word, (through that same pastor): "For the Lord, thy God would say unto you, I have not put you on a shelf, you put yourself on a shelf. For I have called you, and I have placed you in ministry."

> ***All that the Father giveth Me shall come to Me; and him that cometh to Me, I will in no wise cast out.***
> ***John 6:37 KJV***

CHAPTER TWELVE
UNWISE COUNSEL

Through conversations with other abused women, I discovered that at some point in time, we had all been told by some minister that we were being abused by our husbands because we weren't being submissive enough. It was "counsel" given without regard for the safety and well-being of the women or their children.

Unfortunately, this kind of reckless "counsel" has set many women up for a very real struggle with possible rejection by the church for being divorced or separated, even though their spouse is abusive (whether in or out of ministry leadership). It has forced some to do one of two things: either leave the church completely or make the foolish decision to stay in the abusive relationship in order to satisfy the church, at the risk of possibly losing their lives.

Their struggle is not without merit. Christians know very well the Lord's view on separation and divorce, but they somehow overlook the fact that God not only hates divorce but **HE HATES ABUSE AS WELL.**

> *For the Lord, the God of Israel, says, "I HATE divorce and marital separation AND HIM WHO COVERS HIS GARMENT (HIS WIFE) WITH VIOLENCE. Therefore keep a watch upon your spirit (that it may be controlled by My Spirit), that you deal not treacherously and faithlessly [with your marriage mate].*
> *Malachi 2:16 (AMP)*

With that valuable piece of information left out of pulpits across America, many women are sent back into dangerous environments day after day. I grew up traveling in a military family, and I have had the privilege of being a member of many churches across the United States and overseas. The church of which I am presently a member is the *only* church where I've actually heard the pastors speak against abuse and violence in the home.

Let's discuss this question of submission. Even men who are not Christians are aware that the Bible says women are to be submissive to their husbands… (Colossians 3:18). But they will usually ignore or place little to no emphasis on the very next verse which says, "Husbands, love your wives, and do not be harsh with them (Colossians 3:19). This verse, as well as Ephesians 5:28-29, explain how a husband is to behave toward his wife in keeping the marriage covenant.

When my husband challenged me regarding the subject of submission to him as my husband, he also asked me, "How do you submit to the Lord? That's how you are to submit to me."

I thought for a moment. This was a subtle attempt to put me in bondage to this violent relationship, with the use of scripture. The Lord spoke to my heart: Wives submit yourselves to your own husband, AS UNTO THE LORD (Ephesians 5:22).

Those last words in that verse were magnified to me, along with the fact that the previous verse (Ephesians 5:21) states that we were to submit to **one another** in honor to Christ.

The Lord quickened in my heart the fact that if I were required to submit to my husband as unto the Lord, and he was to love me as Christ loves the church, then I should be able to expect the same nurturing and tenderness from my husband as I had grown accustomed to from the Lord.

My reply to my husband was: "If I am to submit to you with the same attitude as in my relationship with the Lord, then you must treat me as He does. And I must admit that the Lord has never hit me, or punched me, or kicked me around as you have."

When abuse occurs in a Christian family, it is a common problem to see blatant misuse of scripture. It occurred to me, in that instant, that the Lord does not require any Christian to put up with abuse in the home. Ephesians 5:24 does not give a man blanket permission to mistreat his wife, especially when verse 25 declares that the love of the husband should be like the love that Jesus has for the church, His bride. The love of Jesus made Him willing to **DIE FOR HER.**

Remember when I mentioned earlier about the problem of people taking positions of authority in the clergy before their minds are renewed in many areas? Well, that can be one of the reasons why so many of us were advised to *go back and take more abuse in the name of submission.* When Romans 12:2 talks about renewing the mind, it means that our thinking is to CHANGE from the way the rest of the world thinks. We are to began to think like God thinks, even if that means forgetting what we've always been told, especially if what you have been told is not what God says.

Just as there are men outside the church who feel they are justified when they abuse their wives, there are men in the clergy who have the same feelings. Just as there are men in the world who feel they have good reasons to abuse their wives, there are men in the clergy who feel the same.

Just as there are men in the world who feel that their wives should "put up" with their violent outbursts, there are men in the clergy who feel the same. Just as there are men in the world who try to excuse their violent behavior by blaming their wives, there are men in the clergy who feel the same.

Pick your counselors wisely and prayerfully. Make up your mind, in advance, that you will not act upon any advice that does not agree with the Word of God. If you've been abused, began to see yourself as God sees you. There is **nothing** in the Word that says, "thou shalt be a door mat." Realize that you are special to God; He keeps a record of the number of hairs on your head. God says that whoever touches you touches the apple of His eye (Zechariah 2:8).

CHAPTER THIRTEEN
CONSTANT HOPE

The first question people ask when they discover that a woman is in an abusive marriage is: "Why don't you leave him?" There can be so much confusion in the mind of a believer over this issue. It's hard to know how long is too long to stay in a relationship where the environment has become violent and dangerous. Make no mistake about it, whenever there is violence, the situation is dangerous and your very life is threatened. If you know that your life is threatened, you've overstayed your time.

There are some good reasons why leaving is usually not the first option, or maybe not even considered by so many Christian women. We all know the Bible teaches that all things, not *some* things, but *all* things, are possible with God. Luke 1:45, says, "And blessed is she that believed: for there shall be a performance of those things which were told her from the Lord" (KJV). A Christian that really believes that nothing is impossible with God, will not leave. And sometimes, many times, women stay in a dangerous situation too long.

They do not seem to understand that God's promises are effective, even if it means waiting for the manifestation at a safe distance. God watches over His Word to see that it is fulfilled (Jeremiah 1:12). That is His job. Your job is to continue in faith (James 1:6).

The Bible says that God hates divorce (Malachi 2:16). Separation, even a temporary separation, can be viewed as a first step in that direction. A Christian that really desires to live by the Bible wants to avoid even the possibility of putting the wheels in motion that may lead toward divorce.

Is there hope? Is there help? Is there deliverance? Yes. Yes. Yes. Every place there is a need, God is available to give aid, healing, and deliverance. But ladies, God is just as able to deliver your husband while keeping you at a safe distance.

> **The prudent see danger and take refuge,**
> **But the simple keep going and suffer for it.**
> **Proverbs 27:12 (NIV)**

Remember when the devil tried to convince Jesus to put Himself in harm's way? (Matthew 4:5-7) They both knew the angels could immediately be dispatched to protect Him. However, Jesus replied, with the established Word, that He would not *tempt* God.

One night, I got a call from the emergency room of one of the local hospitals. Upon arrival, I found a friend of mine, also a minister's wife, who was bruised and disfigured. She had obviously been beaten.

The physician had refused to release her until she found somewhere else to go other than her home, especially since she had refused to press charges. He informed us that several hours before my friend had arrived, another minister's wife had come in to be treated for similar injuries. She admitted that she had been beaten by her husband, and she had also refused to press charges. She had explained to the physician why it was so important for her to return to her home.

Naturally, she had been concerned about the fact that the members of the church would come to visit her in the hospital, and of course, they would ask questions. They might find out what was really happening in her home.

She had further explained that she was praying and believing God, for she had faith and a constant hope that He could and would deliver. The physician, although reluctant, said he had no other choice. He treated and released her. However, one hour later, she was readmitted, this time DOA, (dead on arrival). When she had returned to her home, she was beaten to death by her husband.

> **The prudent see danger and take refuge,**
> **But the simple keep going and suffer for it.**
> **Proverbs 27:12 (NIV)**

My friend was not released from the hospital, until she agreed to come home with me. People, do not tempt God by putting yourself and keeping yourself in harm's way. God can deliver, but the abuser - the one who is inflicting the harm - has to desire to be delivered. You cannot do that for them. That desire has to come from their own heart.

Perhaps the better question to ask here is, how long is too long and how do you know for sure? When you know you are in danger, it's time to go. Your spouse may not have murderous intent, but in a violent situation, very often people are hurt, crippled, and even killed accidentally.

For those of you in ministry leadership, I realize that even the possibility of public exposure of such a serious problem can be very discouraging. What I finally learned is protecting your "privacy" and reputation is not worth risking your health, the emotional stability of both you and your children, and yes, maybe even your life.

CHAPTER FOURTEEN
EXPRESSION OF LOVE?

The heart is deceitful above all things, and
desperately wicked: who can know it?
I the Lord search the heart, I try the reins,
even to give every man according to his
ways,
and according to the fruit of his doings.
Jeremiah 17:9-10 (KJV)

God is love and His conduct toward us is the expression of His love. However, abuse is an expression of hate, and hate is a destructive force. I saw that so clearly one night while reading the experience of Tamar, David's daughter, in 2 Samuel 13. Her brother Amnon, plotted to seduce her because he said he loved her (v. 4). But, the Word says, even though he <u>said</u> he loved her, he raped her, then had her thrown out because he "hated her more than he had loved her" (vs. 15).

An abusive spouse will also say he loves his wife deeply,

but his actions contradict his words. Some husbands say, the reason they wish to have sex with their wives after the abuse, is to show her how much he really loves her. Amnon's sexual and physical abuse of his sister was certainly not a demonstration of love. Neither was the behavior of her father, David, who was made aware of the incident, was very angry about it (2 Samuel 13:21), but never seemed to have time to do anything about it.

During a marriage counseling session, one wife said that her husband only abused her when he had been drinking. Due to the fact that he was drunk, she believed he couldn't control himself. But the husband later admitted that he would get drunk so that he could have an excuse for beating her.

He was admitting that he made the choice to willingly sin against God, and his own flesh (his wife). He chose to be in rebellion and in this particular case, as with my husband, this man also chose to remain in that rebellion.

As water reflects a face, so a man's heart reflects the man. Proverbs 27:19 (NIV)

Marriage turned violent is emotionally destructive because a deep trust is destroyed. Just as Tamar trusted her brother to treat her in the manner that a brother should treat a sister, so does a wife trust her husband to treat her in the manner that a husband should treat a wife. A wife should be able to trust her husband to love her as much as he says he does, because "… husbands ought to love their wives as their own bodies" (Ephesians 5:28).

Unfortunately, what he says with his mouth may not be what is really in his heart. According to Jeremiah 17:10, not only does the Lord search the hearts of men, but He also evaluates conduct in relation to what He finds there. In other words, not only should a man's mouth say, "I love you," but the way he treats you should say, "I love you," as well.

CHAPTER FIFTEEN
EXAMINE YOURSELF

> *... The Lord does not look at the things man looks at. Man looks at the outward appearance, but the Lord looks at the heart.*
> *1 Samuel 16:7b (NIV)*

The two questions I'm asked most frequently are: how can something like this happen in the church and was my former husband saved, was he really a Christian? I don't like to be asked these questions. Rather than just give an opinion, let me get you to think with me for a moment if you will. I believe it will help me to answer both questions at once.

How many times have we seen people make decisions for Christ and take off sharing their faith, winning souls, at church almost every night, working, working, working? Before you know it, they've started a ministry, they're on radio and TV, and on the story goes. We've all seen or at least heard the testimonies of hundreds of ministers with similar stories. We think it's great that these people have grown so fast and are doing the work of the Lord, winning souls into the kingdom.

My former husband had an alcohol and drug abuse problem as a teenager, yet he began preaching at the age of 19, not many months after rededicating his life to the Lord.

Such is the case. So many people jump out of the world and into the pulpit with areas in their lives in which their minds are not yet renewed. That's how we end up with people in the pulpit *and* the pews who still have ideas, opinions, and attitudes that do not line up in agreement with what we know the Word of God teaches. We are too quick to put novices in ministry leadership who are not yet ready, and who may not even meet the qualifications so clearly specified in the Word.

We have Christians that gamble, and abuse themselves (also a sin) by smoking, overeating, and other harmful habits, including abusive natures. In other words, we have Christians that are just like the ones we read about in the Bible. You know - the ones with problem areas in their lives.

It's easy to ask how can these things happen, rather than admit that these things do occur and continue for so long because of situations similar to the case of the Corinthians. Many times, Christians that are around a brother or sister who is practicing sin will talk about it, but will not do the right thing about it.

A very clear example of this is found in 1 Corinthians 5. Paul wrote the church about the sinful conduct of two members of that congregation. The whole church knew about the situation. In fact, they had talked about it so much that Paul had heard about it all the way in Philippi. Yet, they failed to take Godly action toward either person involved (vs 9-13).

First, examine **_yourself_**. I'm sure if you'll examine yourself, you'll find that you may have a problem area in your own life. Perhaps your problem is not even related to abuse, battery, adultery, or abandoning your family, but you've got a problem. It's so easy to condemn someone else when we are made aware of sin in their life, but in my case, the Lord had me to work on myself first, before pointing a finger at anyone else - even the one mistreating me. Continually examine yourself while attending to the needs of a weaker brother who may be in error.

However, it is not possible for a Christian to continually practice sin unless he has fallen into rebellion. This was one of several heart-breaking truths I had to face in my own situation. For example, it never occurred to me that my husband had fallen into total rebellion against God until one morning, while I was watching a Christian television program.

A minister read 1 Samuel 15:23:

> **_For rebellion is as the sin of witchcraft, and stubbornness is as iniquity and idolatry (KJV)_**

There was no question about my husband's rebellion against the things of God, but I had not noticed before that the Bible equated rebellion with witchcraft. Witchcraft was one of the major problems we were dealing with in our congregation. The devil will not turn against himself (Mark 3:23, 26), and in a sense, my husband had joined forces with him by yielding to the same spirit we were dealing with everyday at the church. No wonder we were having so many problems.

Paul told the Christians in Ephesus, "neither *give place* to the devil" (Ephesians 4:27). The devil doesn't have a place in the life of a Christian unless we give him a place. Adam and Eve lost their place of dominion when they *gave it* to satan. In addition, Paul also wrote to the church in Rome:

> *Don't you know that when you OFFER yourselves to someone to obey him as slaves, you are slaves to the one whom you obey whether you are slaves to sin, which leads to death, or to obedience, which leads to righteousness?*
> *Romans 6:15-16 (NIV)*

> *Therefore, I urge you, brothers, in view of God's mercy, to OFFER your bodies as living*
> *sacrifices, holy and pleasing to God – this is your spiritual act of worship.*
> *Romans 12:1 (NIV)*

The inference here is clear. Notice the Word says we *offer* ourselves in His service. God does not take us captive. He does not hold us to Himself against our will. Serving God and following His standard of living, including the act of taking responsibility for that decision is a choice - a choice that every believer must make for himself. Anyone who thinks that simply making the decision to serve the Lord is all it takes to live a successful Christian life, has obviously never made that commitment. It takes work.

> *No, I beat my body and make it my slave so that after I have preached to others, I myself will not be disqualified for the prize.*
> *1 Corinthian 9:27 (NIV)*

Satan is the one who holds people in captivity, manipulating them against their will (2 Timothy 2:26). God has always given us a choice. He has given us a will, and will not violate it. In Deuteronomy 30:19, the Lord gives us the option of choosing life or death. Although He encourages us to choose life, He still leaves the decision up to us.

My husband did not seem to realize that I had many opportunities to retaliate against him and cause serious physical harm, but I chose not to hurt him. Clearly, walking in obedience, as opposed to walking in rebellion, was a choice that God had presented to both of us. I chose life, he chose death. At any time, he could have made the same choice by repenting, turning from sin, seeking help for his problem, and choosing God's way of living.

Abusers are given a choice every day. They do not have to continue to be held captive by the enemy. If you are an abuser, you do not have to continue to live with a violent nature. Abuse no longer has to be your way of life. There is hope and help available for you. You can be free, if you are willing to make the sacrifice necessary to gain freedom. It's your choice.

> **In a large house there are articles not only of gold and silver, but also of wood and clay; some are for noble purposes and some for ignoble.**
>
> **If a man cleanses himself from the latter, he will be an instrument for noble purposes, made holy, useful to the Master and prepared to do any good work.**
> **2 Timothy 2:20-21 (NIV)**

CHAPTER SIXTEEN
THE VALUE OF A GOOD PASTOR

And I will give you pastors according to mine heart, which shall feed you with knowledge and understanding.
Jeremiah 3:15 (KJV)

I wish I could say that I walked out of my situation into total victorious living, but that was not the case. I spiraled into a pit of self-condemnation, guilt and feelings of failure as a woman. I hear Christians give awesome testimonies of never backsliding, and of fighting on in spite of everything, but that was not the case with me.

Although I desired to serve God, I was so discouraged that my strength was sapped and my zeal was gone. I would never have made it, if it had not been for the good pastors God gave me.

The children and I had an unpleasant experience with the first church we attended after the separation. The pastor asked me to leave because it seemed as though divorce was inevitable. He said I was not welcomed if things ended in divorce. I explained my situation, he even met and talked with my husband. But that only left him more convinced that the marriage was over. He asked me to consider leaving his church. We left.

******

The children and I began attending a small church on the outskirts of town. My husband and I had adopted this church as a place for us to steal away to for refreshing. It was a place for us to be ministered to after ministering so much to others. This pastor knew that my husband was also a pastor. He and his wife were accustomed to seeing us on occasion, but always together. They never said a word when suddenly, the children and I were attending alone, all the time.

One day, the pastor informed me that they knew all about my situation. We had never spoken about it. The one thing I so greatly appreciated about being a part of that fellowship, oddly enough, was being left alone. I didn't even want anyone to put their arms around me to say they understood or were praying for me. In fact, I was having a real hard time dealing with Christians at that point in my life.

After all, there had been such a scandal, so much gossip and speculation, and unwarranted confrontations by so many believers since the separation. It was all too clear that many were not concerned, just nosey. There were attempts to get certain bits of information out of the children at the day care. I was constantly changing babysitters.

In additional to that, when I took the children out to eat on our family night, we seemed to always run into my husband and his "date." We were still married, and he was still pastoring, yet more than once, the children and I would see him on these "dates" usually openly displaying some form of intimacy with a woman from the church.

While attending this church, divorce ceased to be a threat, by the time the pastor approached me, the divorce was final. The court hearing was still fresh in my mind. It had not been pleasant. My lawyer was angry because there had been attempts to get information from his office concerning what furniture and other items I would be granted.

During the hearing, my husband had been arrogant, insisting that he would sell whatever items I was awarded before I could arrange to pick them up. All I had asked for was the children's beds. In fact, I didn't want anything. I had left with my children, their clothes and not much else. I never went back for the kid's bed. I wanted to be done with all of this. I just wanted peace in my life.

I had become content to sit under the Word and to be left alone. But this pastor had been given Godly insight. He shared with me that the very first time he shook my husband's hand the Lord had shown him that violent spirit. He said that even though he had attempted to meet and talk with him, my husband kept avoiding a meeting. The pastor felt that my husband was aware of what the Spirit had shown him.

Suddenly some very important things made sense to me. My husband had been so adamant about not wanting marriage counseling with a Spirit-filled minister. Naturally, I had suggested this pastor first because my husband did not pastor a charismatic fellowship. We had adopted this church (a charismatic fellowship), as the place for us to be personally, spiritually fed.

We were part of a traditional, denominational church organization. Our home church was of that same tradition, but it was a little different. Our home church is where both of us had received the baptism of the Holy Spirit, learned about healing, etc. However, many of the ministers in our denomination did not believe as we did.

Once my husband realized that the Lord had revealed his problem to this pastor, he didn't want to have anything to do with him. Instead, when I suggested this pastor for counseling, I was accused of having already discussed his problems with the pastor behind his back. Even though it was obvious that my husband knew that his accusations against me were false, I had not previously understood why he was so determined to avoid this particular pastor.

My pastor had more to share. He said the Lord had awakened him and his wife at the same time one night, shortly after the children and I started attending the church.

"We sat straight up in bed," he said, "and we began to see what looked like a movie screen and scenes began to roll by." Those scenes turned out to be the Lord showing them certain abusive episodes I had experienced.

They began to cry. They still could not believe what they had seen. They had stayed in prayer, but had not approached me or my children. They just loved us.

That was exactly what I needed. When they had finally said something, it was in God's perfect timing.

******

As long as eight years after it all ended, shortly after moving to another state, I had to have surgery four times, largely as a result of injuries sustained during that abusive marriage. My heart was gripped with so much fear, not because of the surgeries. God had given me advanced warning and assurance about that. My biggest concern was the fear of falling into bitterness and unforgiveness toward my former husband. I could not believe that I could still be facing such serious repercussions so long after God had brought me out of that situation.

Yielding to feelings of bitterness and unforgiveness would be taking steps backwards, not forward. It was also becoming increasingly more disturbing to me, that I could not seem to shake what I was feeling. My pastor was very busy. Things were happening so quickly. Surgery had already been scheduled and was only a day or two away.

However, my last night at church, before having surgery, God arranged for my pastor to be available with prayer and wise counsel which helped me through that time.

******

You can avoid further abuse in the house of the Lord, if you keep these two thoughts in mind: hold fast to your profession of faith, and do not discount the value of a good pastor, one who is in pursuit of the heart of God. Even though I have been blessed to travel and live in many different places, the Lord has been faithful to supply the needs of my little family by leading us to churches where we have had the benefit of sitting under pastors who were in pursuit of Him.

I could go on and on, sharing experiences, both good and bad, but I want to deposit, into your spirit, what God has taught me.

The Lord has cautioned me to avoid churches where the pastor has a tendency to "lord it over" the people with intimidation, manipulation, and condemnation (the three elements of witchcraft). 1 Peter 5:2-3 is a scriptural gauge God gave me:

> ***Be shepherds of God's flock that is under your care, serving as overseers – not because you must, but because you are willing, as God wants you to be; not greedy for money, but eager to serve; Not lording it over those entrusted to you, you, but being examples to the flock. (NIV)***

My present pastors have a heart after God. They have established a fellowship that lovingly nurtures both me and my children. Find a fellowship that not only meets your needs, but also the needs of your children. Abuse, separation, and divorce leave scars on their lives, as well. You will all need special attention and caring. Make sure that you submit yourself under a pastor that fosters an attitude of sanctification and purification which create an atmosphere for the manifestation of the healing power of God.

CHAPTER SEVENTEEN
GUARD YOUR HEART…

Above all else, guard your heart, for everything you do flows from it.
Proverbs 4:23 (NIV)

My restoration was obviously orchestrated by the Spirit of God. Yet, the very first thing my pastor's wife told me when I met her was these three words, which I share with you: *Guard your heart.*

Once you know the Lord has set you free, it can be so easy for the enemy to put you back into bondage. My dear friend, Sis. Ellis used to always tell me, that God is truly a deliverer, but once He delivers, it is your responsibility to **stay** free. This is true and applies to any problem you have struggled with in your life. Drugs, alcohol, lying, or even being a victim, it's your responsibility to keep walking in freedom.

Concentrate your efforts on Godly living, and walking in righteousness, right-standing before God. Once you're sure that pleasing God is your goal or your primary motive, make that your focus. Otherwise, you will provide a place for self-condemnation, low self-esteem, lack of self-worth, and feelings of hopelessness and helplessness to grow and become strongholds in your life. These are strongholds that will hold you down, and keep you living beneath your privileges in God for years.

Be careful. Don't continue to get into the prayer line every time someone ministers about being abused in the past. Once you are healed, walk in the reality of that healing.

Don't continue to put on the victim's hat every time someone ministers on suffering, hurt, and abuse. The same holds true in the realm of forgiveness.

You have to forgive the same way you live - by faith, not by feelings. Once again, there is no need for you to jump into every prayer line for people who need to forgive someone who has hurt them in the past. Forgive by faith and go from that place of hurt on to the next chapter that God wants to write in your life.

Avoid subtle deceptions. I've found that some psychiatrists, including Christian psychiatrists, encourage abused women to wait until they "feel ready" to forgive the one who has hurt them. They say that God understands that you may not be able to forgive for a while.

This **sounds** good because of anger that can linger for so long within you. The Word plainly teaches it is alright to be angry, but don't forget that it also teaches that when you are angry, do not sin (Ephesians 4:26).

Harboring unforgiveness in your heart is sin. And it is sin that will hurt you. Sin puts a barrier between you and God and hinders you from receiving what He has in store for you. If you remain in unforgiveness, you will continue to remain in bondage to the abusive situation.

That is why I told you that your relationship with God is not based on feelings; it's based upon the *fact* that *God is*. You must forgive in the fashion in which God expects you to live, by faith (Hebrews 11:6). Don't wait for your feelings to catch up with your spirit man. Remember, God recognizes the **intentions** of your heart (Hebrews 4:12).

Avoid foolish conversation (Ephesians 5:4). I actually know people who have asked me things like: did your husband kick you? where did he hit you, etc? It's unfortunate that we live in a media society. People don't even consider the fact that your life was *not another episode of their favorite television series*. They can say things that are both foolish and insensitive. You do not have to answer those questions. What purpose would it serve? Who does it edify? Be wise, even if your friends or relatives are not. Share only what you wish, when you feel led of the Lord to do so.

Guard yourself against sexual deceptions. Just as your husband may have desired intimacy after inflicting abuse, he may also desire to continue that intimacy after separation or divorce. Abuse and adultery usually go hand-in-hand.

All too often, women find out about the adultery, only after the spouse has infected them with a venereal disease. If your marriage has ended, your former spouse no longer has matrimonial privileges. He has abdicated his commitment to the marriage partner as well as the marriage bed. This should not have to be said to Christian women, but I've spoken with far too many women who allow the abuser to distort some scripture to convince them to continue to sleep with him, even after the divorce.

Use wisdom, ladies. Times are too dangerous for you to be a silly and weak-willed woman (2 Timothy 3:6). Do not tempt God by putting yourself in harm's way. Face the fact that once your spouse has left the home, (either through separation or divorce), there is a very high possibility of adulterous activity. And there is no known cure for some of the things you could be exposed to as a result (i.e. Hepatitis & AIDS).

CHAPTER EIGHTEEN
LEARN TO...

*L**earn to encourage yourself.*** In spite of the magnitude of the problem, God allowed no time for a pity party. As I began to hit bottom, this verse jumped out at me:

> *Why are you downcast, O my soul? Why so disturbed within me? Put your hope in God, for I will yet praise him, my Savior and my God.*
> *Psalms 42:5 (NIV)*

Yes, it was hard to keep going. I had children to feed, a house to clean, clothes to wash, and other responsibilities that could not be neglected. I wanted to have a "pity party" and there was no time for it. I wanted to cry, and there was no time for that, either. It would have been nice to be alone to think things through, or not to think at all. But such was not to be the case.

So often, I wanted someone to talk to, to pour out my heart to, who understood what I was going through. But I never found anyone who could explain why this was happening or what to do. Yet, the Bible seemed to indicate that keeping myself encouraged was my job.

> ***…But David encouraged himself in the Lord his God. 1 Samuel 30:6 (NIV)***

The Holy Spirit has never let me forget that responsibility. I've learned that unless you keep yourself encouraged, the spirit of heaviness (depression) will take over your life.

Learn to recognize God as your source. So many people remain in an abusive relationship for many reasons. They feel they have nowhere to go. They feel they cannot support their children alone. They feel they won't be able to afford day care or educational training for employment. All I know is, God supplied my every need. The more I trusted Him, the more He supplied. The children and I have more today, spiritually and materially, than we ever had during my marriage. Trust God as your source of supply.

Learn to praise God in the midst of your circumstances. While praying late one night, I began to survey my circumstances. I found myself in an $85 a month, dumpy apartment. I was alone with two small children, who were asleep on a broken old couch - our only piece of furniture. Needless to say, my heart began to sink. But the Holy Spirit brought back to my remembrance one of my favorite verses:

> ***In everything give thanks: for this is the will of God in Christ Jesus concerning you. 1 Thessalonians 5:18 (KJV)***

No, I did not feel like praising at the time. But I stood up in the middle of that living-room and began to thank the Lord. At first, it was very weak, but I continued to lift my hands and praise, out loud. The more I thanked Him, the more things the Holy Spirit showed me that I could be thankful for, regardless of the circumstances. Before I knew it, the joy of the Lord, not happiness, which is based on happenings, but the joy of the Lord, gave strength to me.

As I have continued to walk in praise, the Lord has continued to walk us out of the circumstances of defeat and on to new beginnings.

CHAPTER NINETEEN
IN CONCLUSION

But without faith it is impossible to please Him; for he that cometh to God must believe that He is, and that He is a rewarder of them that diligently seek Him.
Hebrews 11:6 (KJV)

Every Christian I have met that has lived through this experience, have all asked the same question, (especially when the situation did not turn out the way they prayed it would): Where was God?

… For He God Himself has said, I will not in any way fail you nor give you up nor leave you without support. I will not, I will not, I will not in any degree leave you helpless nor forsake, nor let you down (relax My hold on you)!….
Hebrews 13:5 (AMP)

The Word is Jesus. So every time the Holy Spirit pulls a scripture up from your memory bank, that's your assurance that He is right there, as promised.

> ***In the beginning was the Word...and the Word was God. John 1:1***
> ***And the Word was made flesh, and dwelt among us. John 1:14 (KJV)***

About four years after the divorce, I began to fully understand why my marriage was not restored as I had prayed. The Lord made it clear to me that He would never override my husband's will.

Both of us had choices to make, and since light and darkness cannot dwell together, when I chose to trust God in the situation and my husband did not ***those decisions divided us***.

So, where was God? Looking back over everything with me, I hope you can see that He was there all the time, faithful to His Word. He was faithful to His promise that He would never leave me or forsake me. The Holy Spirit was faithful to teach me, lead me, and comfort me. He was also faithful to remind me of the Word deposited within me (John 14:26).

> ***The Holy Spirit will bring all things to your remembrance.........***

So, where was God? He was there all the time, giving both you and your spouse the opportunity to walk in harmony with Him and with His will.

If after all of your praying and believing; you've found yourself alone. If, as in my case, you were left feeling as if God did not deliver: **BE ENCOURAGED**. Continue to choose God. Choose life. He delivers, ***even if He doesn't deliver:***

__Let us hear the conclusion of the whole matter: Fear God, and keep His commandments: for this is the whole duty of man.__
__Ecclesiastes 12:13 (KJV)__

ABOUT THE AUTHOR

Marilyn Joyce helps people create strategies and find resources to rebuild their lives after abuse, tragedy, crisis, setbacks, and chronic illness.

Marilyn travels, writes columns, and uses print and digital media to share her recovery strategies to help people rebuild their lives after tragedy, crisis, abuse, setbacks, and chronic illness. After her escape from an abusive marriage, Marilyn was homeless, living in a car with 2 children. Yet, she kept moving forward; attending college while homeless and eventually receiving a direct commission as an Army nurse officer.

While in the Army, Marilyn attended a domestic violence nursing forum where directors of domestic violence shelters shared their difficulties with and concerns for victims from religious communities. That inspired Marilyn to start donating her book of encouragement: **'If He Doesn't Deliver; Domestic Violence in the Religious Home'** to shelters and churches everywhere she traveled with the military.

Before long, Marilyn was speaking for multiple civic groups, universities, conventions, seminars, abuse shelters, churches, and welfare to work organizations. She has spo-

IF HE DOESN'T DELIVER

ken at numerous conferences, including the Annual International Women's Conference in Honolulu, Hawaii with renowned speakers such as Wendy Treat, Cheryl Prewitt-Salem (Miss America 1980, author, singer), Carolyn Savelle, Helen Burns, and Cindy Harrison (wife of Bob Harrison, founder of Christian Business Leaders International).

Marilyn was the producer and host of 'In the Purpose Zone' radio talk show. She was co-host of *Heartlight* talk show KWHE TV Hawaii, featured guest on CBN (*The 700 Club*), guest appearances on NBC, ABC, Watchmen Broadcasting, LeSEA television, and multiple radio outlets, and a segment on CBS Midday news for 5 years.

'Marilyn Joyce was a regular contributor to News 12 Midday. Her monthly appearances offer insight and a wealth of knowledge, especially to the people who are rebuilding their lives and are concerned about their home-based businesses. She uses great examples to get her points across and our viewers look forward to her segments. It's a

pleasure to have her as a guest'. Tom Campbell
'Survive, Get a Life, and Do Your Destiny'
Marilyn Joyce

Marilyn Joyce * 4115 Columbia Rd, Ste 5359 * Martinez, GA 30907-0410
www.ThePurposeZone.com
www.TheJNewsWeekly.com

The National Domestic Violence Hotline
1-800-799-7233 OR 1-800-787-3224 (TTY)

Made in the USA
Columbia, SC
04 July 2021